*In memory of the greatest grandmother who never was,*

*Kathleen Marie Alker.*

Place a photo of your
Grandma Angel here

# My Grandma Angel

When your Grandma Angel was a little girl she was very *small*,
but she knew one day she would *grOW* to do it all.

She dreamed **BIG** dreams
about the places she would go,
the people she would meet,
and the knowledge she would know.

She ate all her greens.

She washed behind her ears.

She did all her homework,

and saved all her tears.

You never know when you might need a tear.

You don't want to run out!

And so she grew **BIG** and tall...

She went to college to find **BIGGER** books.

She traveled the world to see how it looks.

She learned serious business
and why the world is rOund.

She learned every number and
why what goes up must come down.

With all of the knowledge

of the things that she knew,

the whole world wanted Grandma Angel

to do the things she could do.

She could have been an astronaut,

a pilot or a star.

She could have tamed tigers or raced a fast car.

Of all of the things that Grandma Angel could be,

what she wanted most

was to be a mommy for me.

So she had to find Grandpa Angel.

It is very difficult to find

your one husband or wife,

you must look very hard,

sometimes your whole life...

But they found each other!

Together Grandpa and Grandma Angel built it all,

many children in one house

and two puppies with one ball.

It is very important to learn to share.

Grandma Angel was the best mom in the WHOLE

world.

We danced and we played and we whirled and we

twirled.

And I always wondered how lucky I could be,

that the best mom in the world was sent directly to me!!

We went on adventures to Africa and France.

We sang every song and danced every dance.

We sailed the seas and soared the skies.

She showed me the world with my very own eyes.

She taught me to dream **BIG** dreams

about the places I would go,

the people I would meet,

and the knowledge I would know.


And so I grew **BIG** and tall,

just like your Grandma Angel,

who did it all.


I followed her steps and took some of my own.

When my feet took me far away

they always brought me back home.

One day,

when I was grown,

your Grandma Angel told me,


"Today you know all you should know.

You've seen all you need to see,

and you've grown all you can grow.

You can now be the best mommy in the world

for your own little boy or little girl."

See, there are a lot of children who are not as
lucky as you and me.
They never had a mommy to show them all the
things they could be.


So we decided,
your Grandma Angel and me,
that she should show other children
the same MAGIC she showed me.

So with that, a little of her MAGIC

and a really big kiss,

Grandma Angel hopped on a cloud

to go help other kids.

The leaving time is the saddest time.

I'm sure you know this.

You have left someone before,

and there are things that you miss.

But a couple of things are important to know,

everyone must leave to go

the places they will go.

To see the world, you have to be brave,

but to come home is easy

your feet know the way!

Grandma Angel took her Magic and flew to the sky,

to watch from the clouds each day

and from the moon each night.

If you look to the full moon,

you may see her looking down,

she always wears a smile,

unless you're looking upside-down.

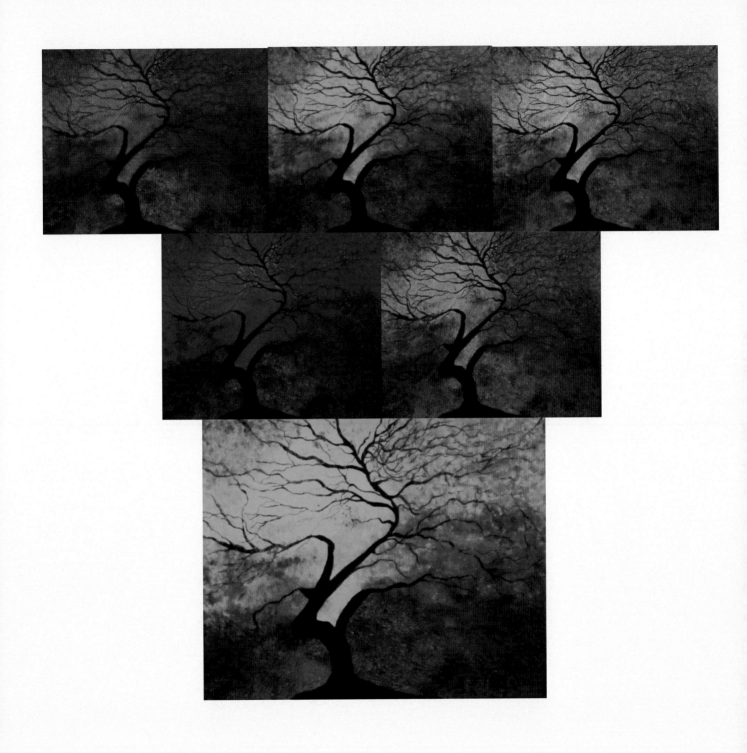

Before she left she told me the rules... 1.2.3.

**One**. Never give-up.

**Two**. Always smile.

**Three**. I always will love my grandbaby.

But most important to remember,
because it is the most important of all,
is to give grandbaby a kiss from me each Night
until grandbaby is BIG and tall.

Made in the
USA
Columbia, SC